Unicorn Coloring Book

Adorable and beautiful unicorns, cute traveling unicons in many countries in the world and more...

Several Pictures of cute unicorns for coloring

(+90 COLORING PAGES)

This Book Belongs To

NEW ZEELAND

PERU

AMERICAN
INDIANS

HAWAII

IRELAND

SWITZERLAND

GREECE

NORWAY

ROMANIA

AUSTRALIA

SAUDI ARABIA

CANADA

ARGENTINA

SPAIN

ITALY

SOUTH AFRICA

FRANCE

UNITED KINGDOM

GERMANY

TURKEY

JAPAN

EGYPT

MEXICO

RUSSIA

BRAZIL

NIGERIA

USA

INDONESIA

INDIA

CHINA

BEACH
BEACH

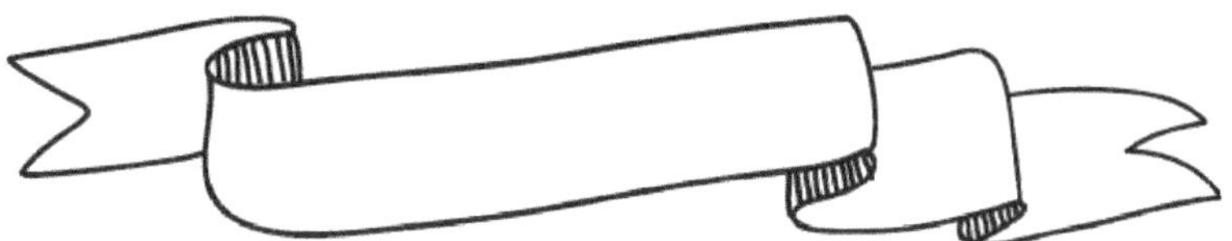

Enjoyed coloring this coloring book?
Discover more books by searching:
(ZiZ Coloring Studio) on amazon.com

www.ingramcontent.com/pod-product-compliance
Lightning Source LLC
Chambersburg PA
CBHW081611250726
48657CB00009B/2538